THE DARKNESS AROUND US IS DEEP

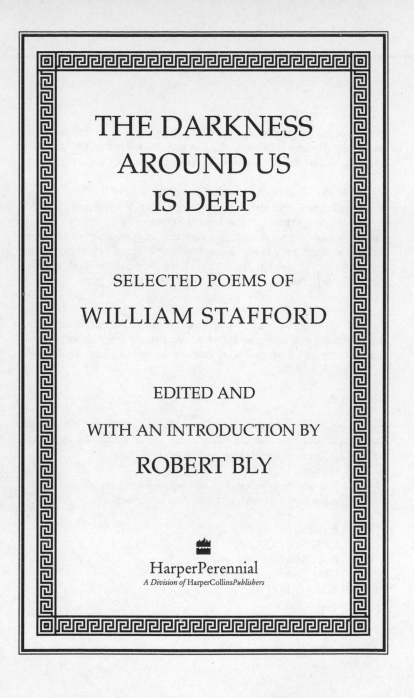

THE DARKNESS
AROUND US
IS DEEP

SELECTED POEMS OF
WILLIAM STAFFORD

EDITED AND

WITH AN INTRODUCTION BY

ROBERT BLY

HarperPerennial
A Division of HarperCollins*Publishers*

These poems originally appeared in *Allegiances; The Rescued Year; Passwords; Traveling Through the Dark; Stories That Could Be True; Someday, Maybe; An Oregon Message;* and *A Glass Face in the Rain.*

HarperCollins books may be purchased for educational, business, or sales promotional use. For information, please write: Special Markets Department, HarperCollins Publishers, Inc., 10 East 53rd Street, New York, NY 10022.

FIRST EDITION

Designed by George McKeon

Library of Congress Cataloging-in-Publication Data
Stafford, William, 1914–
   The darkness around us is deep: selected poems of William Stafford/edited and with an introduction by Robert Bly.
      p.   cm.
      Includes index.
      ISBN 0-06-055328-6
      ISBN 0-06-096916-4 (pbk.)
      I. Bly, Robert.   II. Title.
PS3537.T143A6   1993
811'.54—dc20   93-20696

93 94 95 96 97 ❖/HC 10 9 8 7 6 5 4 3 2 1
   07 ❖/RRD(H) 20 19 18 17   (pbk.)

CONTENTS

INTRODUCTION:
WILLIAM STAFFORD AND THE GOLDEN THREAD
vii

ONE:
FAMILY AND CHILDREN
1

TWO:
TRAVELING THROUGH THE DARK
15

THREE:
SPEAKING THE NATIVE AMERICAN PART IN HIM
39

FOUR:
MOTHER'S VOICE AND FATHER'S VOICE
63

FIVE:
RESCUING SOME YEARS IN KANSAS
83

SIX:
THE REFUSAL TO SERVE WAR
107

INDEX OF POEMS
137

INTRODUCTION:
WILLIAM STAFFORD
AND THE GOLDEN THREAD

1.

William Stafford is a master. He belongs to that category of artists the Japanese have named "national treasures." He offers the work of art as well as sharp ideas about the craft. One of his most amazing gifts to poetry is his theme of the golden thread. He believes that whenever you set a detail down in language, it becomes the end of a thread . . . and every detail—the sound of the lawn mower, the memory of your father's hands, a crack you once heard in lake ice, the jogger hurtling herself past your window—will lead you to amazing riches.

William Blake said,

> *I give you the end of a golden string,*
> *Only wind it into a ball,*
> *It will lead you in at Heaven's gate*
> *Built in Jerusalem's wall.*

I asked Stafford one day, "Do you believe that every golden thread will lead us through Jerusalem's wall, or do you love particular threads?" He replied, "No, every thread." In *Writing the Australian Crawl: Views on the Author's Vocation* (1978), he said, "Any little impulse is accepted, and enhanced. . . . The stance to take, reading or writing is neutral, ready, susceptible to now. . . . Only the golden string knows where it is going, and the role for a writer or reader is one of following, not imposing."

If every detail can by careful handling, through association, sound, tone, language, lead us in, then we live in a sacred universe. Stafford remarked, however, that "purposeful writers" may pull too hard. One has to be careful not to break the thread.

By following the tiny impulses through the meadow of language, the writer may find himself or herself closer to "the self most centrally yours." It would be too much to claim that art, the practice of it, will establish a good, a serene, a superior self. No. But art will, if pursued for itself, bring into realization the "self most centrally yours." Writing poetry, then, doesn't make a poet such as Stafford a better person, only a more genuine *William*.

We note that following the thread is not a passive act. It actually means elaborate mental activity—the longer the line, the more choices we have to make as we near the right margin. The choices are how to follow the thread but not pull it, how to treat associating sounds, emphasize them or let them go, how much assertion is appropriate at each moment. Whether we stay close to the known voice or stretch toward a new voice, whether we come down on the side of aggression or quietism, rebellion or service, we take actions as we follow the thread—or, more accurately, as we follow the thread we immerse ourselves in a flood of action.

Animals are pious, it is said, because they obey their gorgeous limitations. The hawk is always a hawk, even the moment before his death. Hungers remain consistent, such as the owl's for the mouse. The owl does not hanker after the lion's roar, nor does the blue heron hanker after the octopus's elaborate nervous system in his many-minded cave. William Stafford is pious in this wild way. He returns again like a swallow to the barn of yielding, to the little spark of light given off by the end of the thread. We work within limitations, like the owl. "We must accustom ourselves to talking without orating, and to writing without achieving *Paradise Lost*."

2.

New light falls on some of William Stafford's poems when you realize that he is part Indian. This helped me understand an odd quality I had often felt in his poems: his mind almost coincides with the tenets of the white man's world, but not quite. There's even a sense that the fast-moving European way may be only a passing thing. Here is a poem called "Indian Caves in the Dry Country."

> *These are some canyons*
> *we might use again*
> *sometime.*

We begin to notice the several poems in which he speaks to Crazy Horse, or Ishi; in another he prays for the frozen dead at Yellow Knife. He speaks of the Crees as "we"; talks of the Apache word for love; writes "Sioux Haiku":

> *On a relief map*
> *mountains remind my fingers:*
> *"Where Crazy Horse tried."*

Bill's father used to tell the children they were part Crowfoot, a tribe historically known from upstate New York. There is something in his wide-ranging, lively, narrow-lidded way of seeing the world that is not European. It feels prudent, informed, patterned by earth facts, very old.

> The chokecherries along our valley
> still bear a bright fruit. There is good
> pottery clay north of here. I remember
> our old places. When I pass the Musselshell
> I run my hand along those old grooves in the rock.

There is anger at society and its moral stupidities underneath Stafford's poems, and yet one doesn't feel the anger directed at the self that is so much a part of establishment poetry or confessional poetry or leftist poetry. He sees what was lost and what was saved; what was rejected by the Indian community and what was accepted; there's a little distance. No one is wholly at fault, but no one is innocent. "Justice will take us millions of intricate moves."

3.

Many contemporary writers, usefully, study their mothers' and fathers' psyches and feel the weight of these invisible forces pressing them into something smaller than they wished. Stafford in these matters looks to the palpable or hearable. For example, he hears his mother's sharp and sarcastic voice:

> Our mother knew our worth—
> not much. To her, success

was not being noticed at all.
"If we can stay out of jail,"
she said, "God will be proud of us."

"Not worth a row of pins,"
she said, when we looked at the album:
"Grandpa?—ridiculous."

Stafford remarks, "My mother would say abrupt things, reckless things, liberating things. I remember her saying of some people in town, 'They are so boring you get tired of them even when they're not around.'" The poems feel like an extension of family gossip, trenchant statements made to people listening with a little more care than usual. "Something of the tonality of my mother's voice . . . recurs to me now; and I feel the bite of her disappointment in life, and a wry angle of her vision." We can feel that tonality of disappointment in Stafford's voice. Sometimes he'll end a poem with it:

"Yes" means
"Maybe."

Looking like this at you means
"You had your chance."

Stafford experienced his father in a very different way. His father once said to a high school child:

"No need to get home early;
The car can see in the dark."

His father seemed to hear voices from far out in the night. He is described as a listener who encouraged. When William was nine or ten, his father, walking with him in his alert, bird-glimpsing way, remarked, "Now Billy, look carefully in these trees—you may be able to see the hawk better than I can." That's astonishing in this world where so many fathers compete with their sons: "Give me that wrench . . . you're ruining everything."

> *My father heard so much that we still stand*
> *inviting the quiet by turning the face,*
> *waiting for a time when something in the night*
> *will touch us too from that other place.*

Stafford has written many poems about his father, who belonged apparently to that rare group who let their faults be discussed, a great gift to a son. What he heard from his father was "Your job is to find what the world is trying to be." The father's lack of blaming was remarkable. When Stafford's sister wrecked the family car during high school and called home, the father said, "Are you all right?"

We notice that William Stafford never apologizes for a weak poem, but he can easily offer his own poems up for scrutiny or side looks. Talking of his piece on the Sequoia seed, he remarks, "I gave you the poem, mostly just a little evasion, or excursion, then a payoff."

The most helpful advice I ever heard for beginning writers came from Bill during an interview with Cynthia Lofsness, when she was inquiring about his habit of writing a poem every day. She said something like, "What do you do if you're not so good that day?" He said, "Well, then I just lower my standards." The important thing is to adventure your way through language each day, and let blame for weak poems go.

Some critics talk of a poet's body of work as being a conversation between the living poet and some dead person, such as Emerson or Milton. When we read Stafford, we glimpse the possibility that we're hearing two voices, both of which he valued and treasured: his mother's voice and his father's. Perhaps only their child could get them into the same poem.

4.
Of all the American poets of the last thirty years, I think William Stafford broods most about community—the "mutual life" we share, as black people and white people, pacifists and militarists, city people and small-town people.

> *If you don't know the kind of person I am*
> *and I don't know the kind of person you are*
> *a pattern that others made may prevail in the world . . .*

This talks to the value of "inclusiveness," including many people in your world, to the encouragement of diverse voices, listening to the powerful and powerless. Why is it important that we listen?

> *For there is many a small betrayal in the mind,*
> *a shrug that lets the fragile sequence break*
> *sending with shouts the horrible errors of childhood*
> *storming out to play through the broken dike.*

He refers to the abuse that children take from adults— which Alice Miller wrote of so cogently in *For Your Own*

Good—and remarks that this "small betrayal" can be a "shrug," but it is powerful enough to destroy the mutual agreements on which a just society depends.

Then he offers an astonishing image. He notes that elephants parade each holding the other's tail:

> *but if one wanders the circus won't find the park.*

I would have thought "they won't find their way home," but for Stafford it's "the park," the place near the center of town where the whole community plays. When the Staffords lived in Hutchinson, Kansas, their house was only a couple of blocks away from the state fairgrounds.

He offers his idea that the root of all cruelty lies in refusing to recognize what we all know as facts—that others are different from me, that we need to speak who we are, that one person "wandering" can have enormous harmful results. He says we should "consider"—slow down and see what is occurring—"lest the parade of our mutual life get lost in the dark."

He has already covered an immense amount of ground in this poem, and then he goes on to cover more:

> *For it is important that awake people be awake,*
> *or a breaking line may discourage them back to sleep;*
> *the signals we give—yes or no, or maybe—*
> *should be clear: the darkness around us is deep.*

Suddenly we realize another characteristic of William Stafford's work: he wants to talk to people who are awake. When Milton shouts, in a line Stafford has quoted in another context,

Avenge, O Lord, thy slaughtered saints, whose bones
Lie scattered on the Alpine mountains cold,

we could say Milton is shouting to those who are asleep. Much leftist poetry, as well as didactic poetry, is directed to people who are asleep; see Mayakovsky, Robinson Jeffers, Pound's usura canto. Stafford dislikes shouting. "We must accustom ourselves to talking without orating."

We could say that Stafford's calmness, then, flows from his confidence that at least some of us who read him are awake. That confidence probably evokes the courtesy we notice in his poems; to follow him as he follows the golden thread, we have to be awake. If we aren't awake, like so many critics who have—sadly and mistakenly—labeled him as simple, we will complain that we want stronger medicine. By contrast, I like the honor he gives to the intelligence of those who read poetry: "It is important that awake people be awake."

5.

Because William Stafford believes in talking to awake people, he doesn't offer enormous oppositions—Christianity vs. paganism—and then come down heavily, with full artillery, on one side. His habit and his discipline is to think ethically, but he likes to present arguments from both sides, so the poem balances precariously, like a high-wire walker standing on one hand.

If you're driving on a mountain road at night and come on a dead deer, what should you do, go around or stop? Stop only a moment or stop to take action?

Traveling through the dark I found a deer
dead on the edge of the Wilson River road.
It is usually best to roll them into the canyon:
that road is narrow; to swerve might make more dead.

He stops and walks back to the deer, and now the ethical
problem becomes more vivid, pulls in emotion. There is a
live fawn inside.

By glow of the tail-light I stumbled back of the car
and stood by the heap, a doe, a recent killing;
she had stiffened already, almost cold.
I dragged her off; she was large in the belly.

My fingers touching her side brought me the reason—
her side was warm; her fawn lay there waiting,
alive, still, never to be born.
Beside that mountain road I hesitated.

At this moment, he could "swerve," or follow the wrong
elephant. "To swerve might make more dead," as a car
swerving around his parked car could injure strangers. To
be an artist means to discriminate. The artist owes lan-
guage to the human community but owes his or her
breathing body to the animal community. Every poem we
write, every day we live, we think about what we owe to
each. By knowing what to take from the world of culture
and what to give back, what to take from the world of ani-
mals and what to give back, we become adults. That
awake people are aware of the two communities—the
human beings and the animals—is assumed, and the deci-
sion between those two is not easy.

The car aimed ahead its lowered parking lights;
under the hood purred the steady engine.
I stood in the glare of the warm exhaust turning red;
around our group I could hear the wilderness listen.

Ah, yes. The wild things *are* interested in the discriminations a human being makes standing beside his car.

I thought hard for us all—my only swerving—
then pushed her over the edge into the river.

6.

William Stafford looks mild, but actually he is quite fierce. I heard a story about a week he spent as teacher at the Bread Loaf Writers' Conference. The staff emphasized "finding your voice," which turned out to be a study of what the poetry establishment wanted at the moment. Every teacher gave one craft lecture. Stafford began, "I want to say that I don't agree with anything that has been said here this week. You already have a voice and don't need to find one." He hasn't been invited back.

Stafford made a decision in 1942, when he was twenty-eight, to refuse induction in the U.S. Army. Clearly it was a fierce decision. Such refusal brought more consequences in the Second World War than in the Vietnam era. Patriotism ran high in 1942, and the four years Stafford spent working in various objectors' camps put him in danger sometimes from local citizens. His fine prose memoir called *Down in My Heart* describes those four years. And he doesn't apologize, decades later.

In camps like that, if I should go again,
I'd still study the gospel and play the accordion.

He says, in "For My Young Friends Who Are Afraid,"

> *What you fear*
> *will not go away: it will take you into*
> *yourself and bless you and keep you.*
> *That's the world, and we all live there.*

He didn't take that decision—to refuse violence—as a calm man, either. In a disturbing poem called "Clash," he begins:

> *The butcher knife was there*
> *on the table my father made.*
> *The hatchet was on the stair;*
> *I knew where it was.*

He locates the knife and the hatchet not among evil people or in some other country, some other tribe, but in his own house. His mother, it seems, had the hatchet; he had the knife.

> *If she taunted, I grew still.*
> *If she faltered, I lowered the knife.*
> *I did not have to kill.*
> *Time had made me stronger.*

> *I won before too late,*
> *and—a man by the time she died—*
> *I had traveled from love to hate*
> *and partway back again.*

He is not describing any particular family incident here, I think, but a relationship with knife and hatchet that extended over decades. Yet there was one important moment.

> *Now all I have, my life,*
> *strange, comes partly from this:*
> *I thought about a knife*
> *when I learned that great word—"Choose."*

Stafford is not an eccentric thinker who makes up positions as he goes along. Eliot's intellectual matrix was Augustine's certainties around depravity. Wallace Stevens's matrix was Emersonian and Nietzschean certainties around the disappearing gods. Stafford's matrix is clear. He draws from two sources: the rebellious certainties of the Brethren and the pacifists, those who *do*; and the introverted philosophers, those who *think* and *say*.

> *Our vows*
> *cross: never to kill and call it fate.*

He vows he will not kill; he does not call it fate. He compares these vows with every set of impulses that crosses his line of vision. He lays the ideas up next to tiny human events; like a philosopher he is willing also to extend the idea into God's realm and see what happens. When his thought reaches into God's realm, his poetry brushes tragedy:

> *Animals full of light*
> *walk through the forest*

toward someone aiming a gun
loaded with darkness.
That's the world; God
holding still
letting it happen again,
and again and again.

7.

Stafford's decision in 1942 to refuse to be drafted, to refuse to follow the old aggressive patterns, started his adult life. This life—so different in that way from most of ours— began with a right decision. Many began their lives with what was for them a wrong decision. These decisions return one way or another every day. Stafford—distinctively among contemporary poets—faces decisions about aggression in every poem. All those slyly named "decisions" he talks of when he follows the golden thread to the center of the poem amount to refusals to adopt instinctive pressures. "As far as I can assess my own attitudes . . . I have an unusually intense distrust of language." He doesn't want to be led by habit. He wants to make up his own mind whether to mention parking lights or the moon, whether to honor General Patton by bringing him into a poem, or Pascal.

. . . around our group I could hear the wilderness listen.

And the wilderness is interested in what human beings will do, for example, if they pause to think before they respond, and how long they pause. When we give up "orating," we forego collective truths and adopt adventuring in language. When we "decide" we are doing the only possible thing to protect ourselves from interior aggressive patterns.

The reason why William Stafford is such an important poet is that he deals in every poem with discerning, discriminating, particularly how to discriminate between the various responses in us to our own aggressive impulses. We could say that, despite his playful titles, his secret subject is aggression.

A brief glance at infants raging makes clear that the human species is an aggressive species. The human being is aggressive just as water is wet. We know animals—stags or cranes—thrive by a ritualized aggression that ritual controls confer. We abandoned ritual control long ago. Tribal and city culture, human culture as we know it, attempts instead to dampen the aggressive drive in children by taboos, rules, parental tyranny, religious doctrine, by threats of exile or hellfire, by beatings, that usually take place in the family or the school.

Many taboos have recently been abandoned. During the last few decades, more and more barriers to aggression fell away. During the period when Mao, through the Red Guards, actively ordered citizens in China to throw away discrimination and indulge denunciation, violence, destruction of treasures, and the beating of cultured persons, increased shootings, murders, dismemberments, revenge, and mindless killings were being shown on family television in the United States. We could say that mass culture no longer stands in the way of aggression.

How can aggression be controlled? The only other possibility is for each individual member of society to renounce instinctual aggression and choose a peaceful life inside society. "The most stubborn enemies of civilization are its individual members," so the German psychologist Alexander Mitscherlich says. The "driver" inside each human being can, by weighing, balancing, reflecting, pausing, examining, and discriminating, keep his or her own aggressive drives from moving forward into action. Stafford writes in "Lit Instructor" of his work as a teacher:

> Day after day up there beating my wings
> with all of the softness truth requires,
> I feel them shrug whenever I pause:
> they class my voice among tentative things,
>
> And they credit fact, force, battering.
> I dance my way toward the family of knowing,
> embracing stray error as a long-lost boy
> and bringing him home with my fluttering.
>
> Every quick feather asserts a just claim;
> it bites like a saw into white pine.
> I communicate right; but explain to the dean—
> well, Right has a long and intricate name.
>
> And the saying of it is a lonely thing.

This realization that each word we "adventure toward" in a poem involves either giving in to aggression or finding a new way is a weighty one. Poetry is the most playful art of all, and here we see a man bringing serious decision into all this playfulness. That is a wonderful triumph. I believe William Stafford will be read with even greater attention in the next hundred years, because this subject of restraining aggression is the most important problem we face.

PART 1
—————

FAMILY AND
CHILDREN

WITH KIT, AGE SEVEN, AT THE BEACH

We would climb the highest dune,
from there to gaze and come down:
the ocean was performing;
we contributed our climb.

Waves leapfrogged and came
straight out of the storm.
What should our gaze mean?
Kit waited for me to decide.

Standing on such a hill,
what would you tell your child?
That was an absolute vista.
Those waves raced far, and cold.

"How far could you swim, Daddy,
in such a storm?"
"As far as was needed," I said,
and as I talked, I swam.

PASSING REMARK

In scenery I like flat country.
In life I don't like much to happen.

In personalities I like mild colorless people.
And in colors I prefer gray and brown.

My wife, a vivid girl from the mountains,
says, "Then why did you choose me?"

Mildly I lower my brown eyes—
there are so many things admirable people do
    not understand.

AT OUR HOUSE

Home late, one lamp turned low,
crumpled pillow on the couch,
wet dishes in the sink (late snack),
in every child's room the checked,
slow, sure breath—

Suddenly in this doorway where I stand
in this house I see this place again,
this time the night as quiet, the house
as well secured, all breath but mine borne
gently on the air—

And where I stand, no one.

CONSOLATIONS

"The broken part heals even stronger than
    the rest,"
they say. But that takes awhile.
And, "Hurry up," the whole world says.
They tap their feet. And it still hurts on rainy
afternoons when the same absent sun
gives no sign it will ever come back.

"What difference in a hundred years?"
The barn where Agnes hanged her child
will fall by then, and the scrawled words
erase themselves on the floor where rats' feet
run. Boards curl up. Whole new trees
drink what the rivers bring. Things die.

"No good thing is easy." They told us that,
while we dug our fingers into the stones
and looked beseechingly into their eyes.
They say the hurt is good for you. It makes
what comes later a gift all the more
precious in your bleeding hands.

FOR A LOST CHILD

What happens is, the kind of snow that sweeps
Wyoming comes down while I'm asleep. Dawn
finds our sleeping bag but you are gone.
Nowhere now, you call through every storm,
a voice that wanders without a home.

Across bridges that used to find a shore
you pass, and along shadows of trees that fell
before you were born. You are a memory
too strong to leave this world that slips away
even as its precious time goes on.

I glimpse you often, faithful to every country
we ever found, a bright shadow the sun
forgot one day. On a map of Spain
I find your note left from a trip that year
our family traveled: "Daddy, we could meet
    here."

A MEMORIAL: SON BRET

In the way you went you were important.
I do not know what you found.
In the pattern of my life you stand
where you stood always, in the center,
a hero, a puzzle, a man.

What you might have told me
I will never know—the lips went still,
the body cold. I am afraid,
in the circling stars, in the dark,
and even at noon in the light.

When I run what am I running from?
You turned once to tell me something,
but then you glimpsed a shadow on my face
and maybe thought, Why tell what hurts?
You carried it, my boy, so brave, so far.

Now we have all the days, and the sun
goes by the same; there is a faint,
wandering trail I find sometimes, off
through grass and sage. I stop
and listen: only summer again—remember?—

The bees, the wind.

THE LIGHT BY THE BARN

The light by the barn that shines all night
pales at dawn when a little breeze comes.

A little breeze comes breathing the fields
from their sleep and waking the slow windmill.

The slow windmill sings the long day
about anguish and loss to the chickens at work.

The little breeze follows the slow windmill
and the chickens at work till the sun goes
    down—

Then the light by the barn again.

Vacation? Well, our children took our love apart:
"Why do you hold Daddy's hand?" "Susy's
    mother
doesn't have gray in her hair." And scenes
    crushed
our wonder—Sun Valley, Sawtooths, those
    reaches
of the Inland Passage—while the children took
    our
simple love apart.

(Children, how many colors does the light have?
Remember the wide shafts of sunlight, roads
through the trees, how light examines the road
    hour
by hour? It is all various, no simple on-off colors.
And love does not come riding west through the
trees to find you.)

"Daddy, tell me your best secret." (I have woven
a parachute out of everything broken; my scars
are my shield; and I jump, daylight or dark,
into any country, where as I descend I turn
native and stumble into terribly human speech
and wince recognition.)

"When you get old, how do you know what to
   do?"
(Waves will quiet, wind lull; and in that
instant I will have all the time in the world;
something deeper than birthdays will tell me all
   I need.)
"But will you do right?" (Children, children,
oh, see that waterfall.)

LONG DISTANCE

We didn't know at the time. It was
for us, a telephone call through the world
and nobody answered.

We thought it was a train far off
giving its horn, roving its headlight
side to side in its tunnel of darkness
and shaking the bridge and our house
till dishes rattled, and going away.

We thought it a breath climbing the well where
   Kim
almost fell in; it was a breath saying his name,
and "Almost got you," but we piled boards
and bricks on top and held off that voice.

Or maybe it was the song in the stove—
walnut and elm giving forth stored sunlight
through that narrow glass eye on the front
in the black door that held in the fire.

Or a sigh from under the mound of snow where
   Bret's
little car with its toy wheels nestled all winter
ready to roll, come spring, and varoom
when his feet toddled it along.

Or—listen—in the cardboard house
we built by the kitchen wall, a doorknob
drawn with crayon, Kit's little window peeking
out by the table—is it a message from there?

And from Aunt Helen's room where she sews
all day on a comforter made out of pieces of
    Grandma's
dresses, and the suits for church—maybe those
patches rustle their message in her fingers:
"Dorothy, for you, and for all the family I sew
that we may be warm in the house by the
    tracks."

I don't know, but there was a voice,
those times, a call through the world that almost
rang everywhere, and we looked up—Dorothy,
    Helen,
Bret, Kim, Kit—and only the snow
shifted its foot outside in the wind,
and nobody heard.

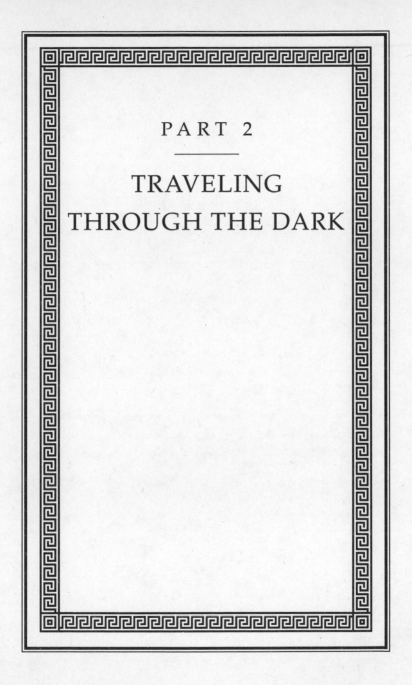

PART 2

TRAVELING
THROUGH THE DARK

BI-FOCAL

Sometimes up out of this land
a legend begins to move.
Is it a coming near
of something under love?

Love is of the earth only,
the surface, a map of roads
leading wherever go miles
or little bushes nod.

Not so the legend under,
fixed, inexorable,
deep as the darkest mine
the thick rocks won't tell.

As fire burns the leaf
and out of the green appears
the vein in the center line
and the legend veins under there,

So, the world happens twice—
once what we see it as;
second it legends itself
deep, the way it is.

A STORY THAT COULD BE TRUE

If you were exchanged in the cradle and
your real mother died
without ever telling the story
then no one knows your name,
and somewhere in the world
your father is lost and needs you
but you are far away.

He can never find
how true you are, how ready.
When the great wind comes
and the robberies of the rain
you stand on the corner shivering.
The people who go by—
you wonder at their calm.

They miss the whisper that runs
any day in your mind,
"Who are you really, wanderer?"—
and the answer you have to give
no matter how dark and cold
the world around you is:
"Maybe I'm a king."

HOW THESE WORDS HAPPENED

In winter, in the dark hours, when others
were asleep, I found these words and put them
together by their appetites and respect for
each other. In stillness, they jostled. They traded
meanings while pretending to have only one.

Monstrous alliances never dreamed of before
began. Sometimes they last. Never again
do they separate in this world. They die
together. They have a fidelity that no
purpose or pretense can ever break.

And all of this happens like magic to the words
in those dark hours when others sleep.

NEAR

Walking along in this not quite prose way
we both know it is not quite prose we speak,
and it is time to notice this intolerable snow
innumerably touching, before we sink.

It is time to notice, I say, the freezing snow
hesitating toward us from its gray heaven;
listen—it is falling not quite silently
and under it still you and I are walking.

Maybe there are trumpets in the houses we pass
and a redbird watching from an evergreen—
but nothing will happen until we pause
to flame what we know, before any signal's
    given.

FOUND IN A STORM

A storm that needed a mountain
met it where we were:
we woke up in a gale
that was reasoning with our tent,
and all the persuaded snow
streaked along, guessing the ground.

We turned from that curtain, down.
But sometime we will turn
back to the curtain and go
by plan through an unplanned storm,
disappearing into the cold,
meanings in search of a world.

A SONG IN THE MANNER OF
FLANNERY O'CONNOR

Snow on the mountain—water in
the valley: you beat a mule and
it works hard, Honey.
   Have a cigarette?

Where is the guidepost? Written on
your hand: you point places with it
and everyone understands.
   Like to dance, Honey?

Country folks used to talk to us
like this. Now they're wiser
than the rest of us.
   So long, Sucker.

IF I COULD BE LIKE
WALLACE STEVENS

The octopus would be my model—
it wants to understand; it prowls
the rocks a hundred ways and holds
its head aloof but not ignoring.
All its fingers value what
they find. "I'd rather know," they say.
"I'd rather slime along than be heroic."

My pride would be to find out; I'd
bow to see, play the fool,
ask, beg, retreat like a wave—
but somewhere deep I'd hold the pearl,
never tell. "Mr. Charley,"
I'd say, "talk some more. Boast again."
And I'd play the banjo and sing.

MY HANDS

It is time for applause. My hands rest
on the balcony railing. They inflict
their silence, lying there innocently.
Or—I may wound people by not shaking hands.
Somewhere a computer saves it up, my
indifference: if I ever meet the performer
our greeting will hover in the subtle gradations.

Sometimes I carry these weapons my hands
quietly to a reception. In their cuffs
they look tame, but I know them and hold them
    still.
When they pick up a glass or a sandwich they
    close
with just enough grip. They are generous,
always alert. And they're mine, terribly
sure, always loyal to me.

AN ARCHIVAL PRINT

God snaps your picture—don't look away—
this room right now, your face tilted
exactly as it is before you can think
or control it. Go ahead, let it betray
all the secret emergencies and still hold
that partial disguise you call your character.

Even your lip, they say, the way it curves
or doesn't, or can't decide, will deliver
bales of evidence. The camera, wide open,
stands ready; the exposure is thirty-five years
or so—after that you have become
whatever the veneer is, all the way through.

Now you want to explain. Your mother
was a certain—how to express it?—*influence.*
Yes. And your father, whatever he was,
you couldn't change that. No. And your town
of course had its limits. Go on, keep talking—
Hold it. Don't move. That's you forever.

RUN BEFORE DAWN

Most mornings I get away, slip out
the door before light, set forth on the dim gray
road, letting my feet find a cadence
that softly carries me on. Nobody
is up—all alone my journey begins.

Some days it's escape: the city is burning
behind me, cars have stalled in their tracks,
and everybody is fleeing like me but some other
    direction.
My stride is for life, a far place.

Other days it is hunting: maybe some game will
    cross
my path and my stride will follow for hours,
    matching
all turns. My breathing has caught the right beat
for endurance; familiar trancelike scenes glide
    by.

And sometimes it's a dream of motion,
    streetlights coming near,
passing, shadows that lean before me,
    lengthened
then fading, and a sound from a tree: a soul, or
    an owl.

These journeys are quiet. They mark my days with
    adventure
too precious for anyone else to share, little gems
of darkness, the world going by, and my breath,
    and the road.

6

Written on the Stub of the First Paycheck

Gasoline makes game scarce.
In Elko, Nevada, I remember a stuffed wildcat
someone had shot on Bing Crosby's ranch.
I stood in the filling station
breathing fumes and reading the snarl of a map.

There were peaks to the left so high
they almost got away in the heat;
Reno and Las Vegas were ahead.
I had promise of the California job,
and three kids with me.

It takes a lot of miles to equal one wildcat
today. We moved into a housing tract.
Every dodging animal carries my hope in
    Nevada.
It has been a long day, Bing.
Wherever I go is your ranch.

AN OREGON MESSAGE

When we first moved here, pulled
the trees in around us, curled
our backs to the wind, no one
had ever hit the moon—no one.
Now our trees are safer than the stars,
and only other people's neglect
is our precious and abiding shell,
pierced by meteors, radar, and the telephone.

From our snug place we shout
religiously for attention, in order to hide:
only silence or evasion will bring
dangerous notice, the hovering hawk
of the state, or the sudden quiet stare
and fatal estimate of an alerted neighbor.

This message we smuggle out in
its plain cover, to be opened
quietly: Friends everywhere—
we are alive! Those moon rockets
have missed millions of secret
places! Best wishes.

Burn this.

ALLEGIANCES

It is time for all the heroes to go home
if they have any, time for all of us common ones
to locate ourselves by the real things we live by.

Far to the north, or indeed in any direction,
strange mountains and creatures have always
    lurked:
elves, goblins, trolls, and spiders—we
encounter them in dread and wonder,

But once we have tasted far streams, touched the
    gold,
found some limit beyond the waterfall,
a season changes, and we come back, changed
but safe, quiet, grateful.

Suppose an insane wind holds all the hills
while strange beliefs whine at the traveler's ears,
we ordinary beings can cling to the earth and
    love
where we are, sturdy for common things.

HOW TO REGAIN YOUR SOUL

Come down Canyon Creek trail on a summer
    afternoon
that one place where the valley floor opens out.
    You will see
the white butterflies. Because of the way
    shadows
come off those vertical rocks in the west, there
    are
shafts of sunlight hitting the river and a deep
long purple gorge straight ahead. Put down your
    pack.

Above, air sighs the pines. It was this way
when Rome was clanging, when Troy was being
    built,
when campfires lighted caves. The white
    butterflies dance
by the thousands in the still sunshine. Suddenly
    anything
could happen to you. Your soul pulls toward the
    canyon
and then shines back through the white wings to
    be you again.

SALVAGED PARTS

Fire took the house. Black bricks
tell how it went. Wild roses
try to say it never happened.

A rock my foot pushed falls
for years down the cellar stairs. . . .
No thanks, no home again for me—

Mine burned before it burned.
A rose pretends, but I always knew:
a rose pretends, a rock tells how it is.

TURN OVER YOUR HAND

Those lines on your palm, they can be read
for a hidden part of your life that only
those links can say—nobody's voice
can find so tiny a message as comes
across your hand. Forbidden to complain,
you have tried to be like somebody else,
and only this fine record you examine
sometimes like this can remember where
you were going before that long
silent evasion that your life became.

You the very old, I have come
to the edge of your country and looked across,
how your eyes warily look into mine
when we pass, how you hesitate when
we approach a door. Sometimes
I understand how steep your hills
are, and your way of seeing the madness
around you, the careless waste of the calendar,
the rush of people on buses. I have
studied how you carry packages,
balancing them better, giving them attention.
I have glimpsed from within the gray-eyed look
at those who push, and occasionally even I
can achieve your beautiful bleak perspective
on the loud, the inattentive, shoving boors
jostling past you toward their doom.

With you, from the pavement I have watched
the nation of the young, like jungle birds
that scream as they pass, or gyrate on
    playgrounds,
their frenzied bodies jittering with the disease
of youth. Knowledge can cure them. But
not all at once. It will take time.

There have been evenings when the light
has turned everything silver, and like you
I have stopped at a corner and suddenly
staggered with the grace of it all: to have
inherited all this, or even the bereavement
of it, and finally being cheated!—the chance
to stand on a corner and tell it goodbye!
Every day, every evening, every
abject step or stumble has become heroic:—

You others, we the very old have a country.
A passport costs everything there is.

TRAVELING THROUGH THE DARK

Traveling through the dark I found a deer
dead on the edge of the Wilson River road.
It is usually best to roll them into the canyon:
that road is narrow; to swerve might make more
  dead.

By glow of the tail-light I stumbled back of the
  car
and stood by the heap, a doe, a recent killing;
she had stiffened already, almost cold.
I dragged her off; she was large in the belly.

My fingers touching her side brought me the
  reason—
her side was warm; her fawn lay there waiting,
alive, still, never to be born.
Beside that mountain road I hesitated.

The car aimed ahead its lowered parking lights;
under the hood purred the steady engine.
I stood in the glare of the warm exhaust turning
  red;
around our group I could hear the wilderness
  listen.

I thought hard for us all—my only swerving—
then pushed her over the edge into the river.

In the late night listening from bed
I have joined the ambulance or the patrol
screaming toward some drama, the kind of end
that Berky must have some day, if she isn't dead.

The wildest of all, her father and mother cruel,
farming out there beyond the old stone quarry
where high-school lovers parked their lurching
    cars,
Berky learned to love in that dark school.

Early her face was turned away from home
toward any hardworking place; but still her soul,
with terrible things to do, was alive, looking out
for the rescue that—surely, some day—would have
    to come.

Windiest nights, Berky, I have thought for you,
and no matter how lucky I've been I've touched
    wood.
There are things not solved in our town though
    tomorrow came:
there are things time passing can never make
    come true.

We live in an occupied country, misunderstood;
justice will take us millions of intricate moves.
Sirens will hunt down Berky, you survivors in
    your beds
listening through the night, so far and good.

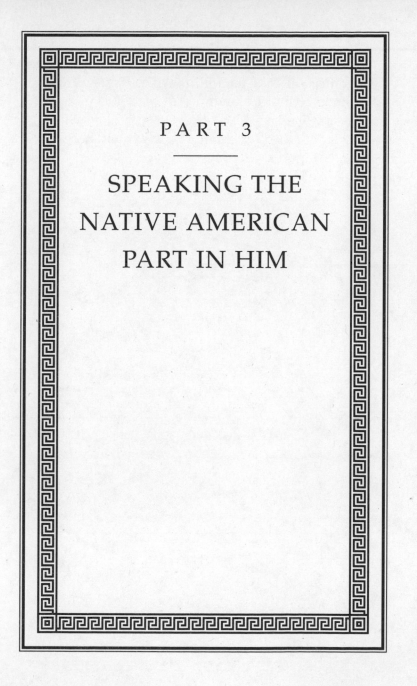

PART 3

SPEAKING THE
NATIVE AMERICAN
PART IN HIM

IN THE OREGON COUNTRY

From old Fort Walla Walla and the Klickitats
to Umpqua near Port Orford, stinking fish tribes
massacred our founders, the thieving whites.

Chief Rotten Belly slew them at a feast;
Kamiakin riled the Snakes and Yakimas;
all spurted arrows through the Cascades west.

Those tribes became debris on their own lands:
Captain Jack's wide face above the rope,
his Modoc women dead with twitching hands.

The last and the most splendid, Nez Percé
Chief Joseph, fluttering eagles through Idaho,
dashed his pony-killing getaway.

They got him. Repeating rifles bored at his head,
and in one fell look Chief Joseph saw the game
out of that spiral mirror all explode.

Back of the northwest map their country goes,
mountains yielding and hiding fold on fold,
gorged with yew trees that were good for bows.

1

A long rope of gray smoke was
coming out of the ground. I went
nearer and looked at it sideways.
I think there was a cave, and some people
were in a room by a fire in the earth.
One of them thought of a person like me
coming near but never quite coming in
to know them.

2

Once a man killed another, to rob him,
but found nothing, except that lying
there by a rock was a very sharp,
glittering little knife. The murderer
took the knife home and put it beside
his bed, and in the night he woke
and the knife was gone. But there was
no way for a person to get in to take the knife.

The man went to a wise old woman.
When she heard the story, she began to laugh.
The man got mad. He yelled at the woman
to tell why she was laughing. She looked
at him carefully with her eyes squinted

as if she looked at the sun. "Can't you
guess what happened?" she asked.

The man didn't want to be dumb, so
he thought and thought. "Maybe the knife
was so sharp that it fell on the ground
and just cut its way deeper and deeper and
got away." The woman squinted some more.
She shook her head. "You learned that from
a story. No, I will tell you why you
thought the knife was gone and why
you came here to ask me about it:
you are dead."

Then the man noticed that he didn't
have any shadow. He went out and
looked around: nothing had any shadow.
He began to squint up his eyes, it was
all so bright. And wherever he looked
there were sharp little knives.

This is a true story. He really was dead.
My mother told us about it. She told us
never to kill or rob.

3
At a little pond in the woods
I decided: this is the center of my life.
I threw a big stick far out, to be
all the burdens from earlier years.
Ever since, I have been walking
lightly, looking around, out of the woods.

IN THE NIGHT DESERT

The Apache word for love twists
    then numbs the tongue:
Uttered once clear, said—
    never that word again.

"Cousin," you call, or "Sister," and one
    more word that spins
In the dust: a talk-flake
    chipped like obsidian.

The girl who hears this flake and
    follows you into the dark
Turns at a touch: the night desert
    forever behind her back.

They called it Neosho, meaning
"a river made muddy by buffalo."
You don't need many words if you
already know what you're talking about,
and they did. But later there was
nothing they knew that made any difference.

I am thinking of those people—say one
of them looks at you; for an instant you see
a soul like your own, and you are both
lost. What the spirit has given
you to do is unworthy. Two kinds of
dirt, you look at each other.

But still, I have waded that river
and looked into the eyes of buffalo
that were standing and gazing far:
no soul I have met knew the source
that well, or where the Neosho
went when it was clear.

They hurt no one. They rove the North.
Owning the wilderness, they're not lost.
They couple in joy; in fear, they run.
Old, their lives move still the same—
all a pattern across the land,
one step, one breath, one. . . .

Winter bundles them close; their fur
bunches together in friendly storms.
Everything cold can teach, they learn.
They stand together. The future comes.

These are some canyons
we might use again
sometime.

When I face north a lost Cree
on some new shore puts a moccasin down,
rock in the light and noon for seeing,
he in a hurry and I beside him.

It will be a long trip; he will be a new chief;
we have drunk new water from an unnamed
    stream;
under little dark trees he is to find a path
we both must travel because we have met.

Henceforth we gesture even by waiting;
there is a grain of sand on his knife blade
so small he blows it and while his breathing
darkens the steel his eyes become set

And start a new vision: the rest of his life.
We will mean what he does. Back of this page
the path turns north. We are looking for a sign.
Our moccasins do not mark the ground.

WIND WORLD

One time Wind World
found a way through the mountains
and called on Sky. Their
child was Thirst, who lives
wherever those two go, and brings
them ragged little dolls he
finds in the desert.

Wind World likes it near
the ground, and hurries there
even on still days, low.
You can see him shaking hands
with himself in the grass.

Wind World always made friends with
us Indians, who wore feathers for him.
Even today when he finds an arrowhead
in the dust or sand
he just leaves it there.

Wind World likes things that
move, but you notice
he has to pass something still
for him really to sing a song.

A Joshua tree near Mojave
told me these things one day
about Wind World.

THE CONCEALMENT: ISHI, THE LAST
WILD INDIAN

A rock, a leaf, mud, even the grass
Ishi the shadow man had to put back where it
     was.
In order to live he had to hide that he did.
His deep canyon he kept unmarked for the
     world,
and only his face became lined, because no one
     saw it
and it therefore didn't make any difference.

If he appeared, he died; and he was the last.
     Erased
footprints, berries that purify the breath, rituals
before dawn with water—even the dogs roamed
     a land
unspoiled by Ishi, who used to own it, with his
     aunt
and uncle, whose old limbs bound in willow
     bark finally
stopped and were hidden under the rocks, in
     sweet leaves.

We ought to help change that kind of premature
     suicide,
the existence gradually mottled away till the
     heartbeat

blends and the messages all go one way from the
  world
and disappear inward: Ishi lived. It was all right
for him to make a track. In California now where his
  opposites
unmistakably dwell we wander their streets.

And sometimes whisper his name—
"Ishi."

PEOPLE OF THE SOUTH WIND

1

One day Sun found a new canyon.
It hid for miles and ran far away,
then it went under a mountain. Now Sun
goes over but knows it is there. And that
is why Sun shines—it is always looking.
Be like the sun.

2

Your breath has a little shape—
you can see it cold days. Well,
every day it is like that, even in summer.
Well, your breath goes, a whole
army of little shapes. They are living
in the woods now and are your friends.
When you die—well, you go with
your last breath and find the others.
And in open places in the woods
all of you are together and happy.

3

Sometimes if a man is evil his breath
runs away and hides from him. When he
dies his last breath cannot find the others,
and he never comes together again—
those little breaths, you know, in the autumn

they scurry the bushes before snow.
They never come back.

4
You know where the main river
runs—well, for five days below is
No One, and out in the desert
on each side his children live.
They have their tents that echo dust
and give a call for their father
when you knock for acquaintance:
"No One, No One, No One."

When you cross that land the sandbars
have his name in little tracks
the mice inscribe under the bushes,
and on pools you read his wide, bland
reply to all that you ask. You wake
from dreams and hear the end of things:
"No One, No One, No One."

REPORT TO CRAZY HORSE

All the Sioux were defeated. Our clan
got poor, but a few got richer.
They fought two wars. I did not
take part. No one remembers your vision
or even your real name. Now
the children go to town and like
loud music. I married a Christian.

Crazy Horse, it is not fair
to hide a new vision from you.
In our schools we are learning
to take aim when we talk, and we have
found out our enemies. They shift when
words do; they even change and hide
in every person. A teacher here says
hurt or scorned people are places
where real enemies hide. He says
we should not hurt or scorn anyone,
but help them. And I will tell you
in a brave way, the way Crazy Horse
talked: that teacher is right.

I will tell you a strange thing:
at the rodeo, close to the grandstand,
I saw a farm lady scared by a blown
piece of paper; and at that place

horses and policemen were no longer
frightening, but suffering faces were,
and the hunched-over backs of the old.

Crazy Horse, tell me if I am right:
these are the things we thought we were
doing something about.

In your life you saw many strange things,
and I will tell you another: now I salute
the white man's flag. But when I salute
I hold my hand alertly on the heartbeat
and remember all of us and how we depend
on a steady pulse together. There are those
who salute because they fear other flags
or mean to use ours to chase them:
I must not allow my part of saluting
to mean this. All of our promises,
our generous sayings to each other, our
honorable intentions—those I affirm
when I salute. At these times it is like
shutting my eyes and joining a religious
colony at prayer in the gray dawn
in the deep aisles of a church.

Now I have told you about new times.
Yes, I know others will report
different things. They have been caught
by weak ways. I tell you straight
the way it is now, and it is our way,
the way we were trying to find.

The chokecherries along our valley
still bear a bright fruit. There is good
pottery clay north of here. I remember
our old places. When I pass the Musselshell
I run my hand along those old grooves in the
    rock.

SIOUX HAIKU

On a relief map
mountains remind my fingers:
"Where Crazy Horse tried."

THE RESEARCH TEAM IN THE
MOUNTAINS

We have found a certain heavy kind of wolf.
Haven't seen it, though—
just *know* it.

Answers are just echoes, they say. But
a question travels before it comes back,
and that counts.

Did you know that here everything is free?
We've found days that wouldn't allow a price
on anything.

When a dirty river and a clean river
come together the result is—
dirty river.

If your policy is to be friends in the mountains
a rock falls on you: the only real friends—
you can't help it.

Many go home having "conquered a
    mountain"—
they leave their names at the top in a jar
for snow to remember.

Looking out over the campfire at night
again this year I pick a storm for you,
again the first one.

We climbed Lostine and Hurricane and Chief
    Joseph canyons;
finally in every canyon the road ends.
Above that—storms of stone.

In the Aztec design God crowds
into the little pea that is rolling
out of the picture.
All the rest extends bleaker
because God has gone away.

In the White Man design, though,
no pea is there.
God is everywhere
but hard to see.
The Aztecs frown at this.

How do you know He is everywhere?
And how did He get out of the pea?

Light wind at Grand Prairie, drifting snow.
Low at Vermilion, forty degrees of frost.
Lost in the Barrens, hunting over spines of ice,
the great sled dog Shadow is running for his life.

All who hear—in your wide horizon of thought
caught in this cold, the world all going gray—
pray for the frozen dead at Yellow Knife.
These words we send are becoming parts of their
    night.

PART 4

MOTHER'S VOICE
AND FATHER'S VOICE

OUR KIND

Our mother knew our worth—
not much. To her, success
was not being noticed at all.
"If we can stay out of jail,"
she said, "God will be proud of us."

"Not worth a row of pins,"
she said, when we looked at the album:
"Grandpa?—ridiculous."
Her hearing was bad, and that
was good: "None of us ever says much."

She sent us forth equipped
for our kind of world, a world of
our betters, in a nation so strong
its greatest claim is no boast,
its leaders telling us all, "Be proud"—

But over their shoulders, God and
our mother, signaling: "Ridiculous."

MY MOTHER WAS A SOLDIER

If no one moved on order, she would kill—
that's what the gun meant, soldier. No one
told you? Her eye went down the barrel; her
    hand
held still; gunpowder paid all that it owed
at once. No need to count the dead.

Hunting, she dragged the bait till nightfall, then
hung it in a tree and waited. Time
was working for her, and the quiet. What a
    world
it is, for thinkers! Contact would come, and
the wildest foe fall fastest, Mother said.

Tapping on my wrist, she talked: "Patience
is the doctor; it says try; it says
they think we're nice, we quiet ones, we die
so well: that's how we win, imagining things
before they happen." "No harm in being quiet,"

My mother said; "that's the sound that finally
    wins."

VACATION TRIP

The loudest sound in our car
was Mother being glum:

> Little chiding valves
> a surge of detergent oil
> all that deep chaos
> the relentless accurate fire
> the drive shaft wild to arrive

And tugging along behind in its great big
  balloon,
that looming piece of her mind:

"I wish I hadn't come."

Peg said, "This one," and we bought it
for Mother, our allowance for weeks
paid out to a clerk who snickered—
a hideous jar, oil-slick in color,
glass that light got lost in.

We saw it for candy, a sign for
our love. And it lasted:
the old house on Eleventh,
a dim room on Crescent where
the railroad shook the curtains,
that brief glory at Aunt Mabel's place.

Peg thought it got more beautiful,
Egyptian, sort of, a fire-sheened
relic. And with a doomed grasp
we carried our level of aesthetics
with us across Kansas, proclaiming
our sentimental badge.

Now Peg says, "Remember that candy jar?"
She smooths the silver. "Mother
hated it." I am left standing
alone by the counter, ready to buy what
will hold Mother by its magic, so
she will never be mad at us again.

You would not want too reserved a speaker—
that is a cold way to live.
But where I come from withdrawal
is easy to forgive.

When Mother was a girl Indians
shadowed that country, the barren lands.
Mother ran to school winter mornings
with hot potatoes in her hands.

She was like this—foreign, a stranger.
She could not hear very well;
the world was all far. (Were the others laughing?
She never could tell.)

Later, though she was frightened,
she loved, like everyone.
A lean man, a cruel, took her.
I am his son.

He was called Hawk by the town people,
but was an ordinary man.
He lived by trapping and hunting
wherever the old slough ran.

Our house was always quiet.
Summers the windmill creaked, or a board.
I carried wood, never touching anyone.
Winters the black stove roared.

Forgive me these shadows I cling to, good
    people,
trying to hold quiet in my prologue.
Hawks cling the barrens wherever I live.
The world says, "Dog eat dog."

Mother, the sweet peas have gushed out of
the ground where you fell, where you lay that day
when the doctor came, while your wash kept
    flapping
on the line across the backyard. I stood
and looked out a long time toward the
    Fairgrounds.
The Victrola in the living room used to play
"Nola," and the room spun toward a center
that our neighborhood clustered around.
    Nasturtiums
you put in our salad would brighten our tummies,
you said, and we careened off like trains
to play tag in alfalfa fields till the moon
came out and you called us home with "Popcorn
for all who come." But that was long
before you said, "Jesus is calling me home."

And Father, when your summons came and you
    quietly
left, no one could hold you
back. You didn't need to talk
because your acts for years had already prayed.
For you both, may God guide my hand in its
    pious
act, from far off, across this page.

"No need to get home early;
the car can see in the dark."
    He wanted me to be rich
    the only way we could,
    easy with what we had.

And always that was his gift,
given for me ever since,
    easy gift, a wind
    that keeps on blowing for flowers
    or birds wherever I look.

World, I am your slow guest,
one of the common things
    that move in the sun and have
    close, reliable friends
    in the earth, in the air, in the rock.

VOCATION

This dream the world is having about itself
includes a trace on the plains of the Oregon trail,
a groove in the grass my father showed us all
one day while meadowlarks were trying to tell
something better about to happen.

I dreamed the trace to the mountains, over the
     hills,
and there a girl who belonged wherever she was.
But then my mother called us back to the car:
she was afraid; she always blamed the place,
the time, anything my father planned.

Now both of my parents, the long line through
     the plain,
the meadowlarks, the sky, the world's whole
     dream
remain, and I hear him say while I stand
     between the two,
helpless, both of them part of me:
"Your job is to find what the world is trying to
     be."

LISTENING

My father could hear a little animal step,
or a moth in the dark against the screen,
and every far sound called the listening out
into places where the rest of us had never been.

More spoke to him from the soft wild night
than came to our porch for us on the wind;
we would watch him look up and his face go
    keen
till the walls of the world flared, widened.

My father heard so much that we still stand
inviting the quiet by turning the face,
waiting for a time when something in the night
will touch us too from that other place.

"The freezing convict wanted
back in the prison. The warden
laughed and let the storm execute
him. The wind mourned."

How often such abrupt
flakes formed around us!—
jabs of ice into lace,
daggers that appeared out of nothing,

So graceful the heart beat
late, could never catch up
again. You imagined a face in the
snow to burn the furnace down, and

"Once a wolf brought sticks
to a beaver—the mountains are
surely that big." Oh, Father, why
did you ever set your son such being!

Your life was a miracle
and could build out of shadows
anything: your restless thought
has made the world haunted;

Your memory like a snowflake forms
out of the night and comes down like
a new star all the time over wolf, storm,
woods, and millions of faces. . . .

"Once a child named 'Remember'
found a forest that wasn't trees, except
for one—named 'Doris Pine.' . . . "
Oh, Father, you always found the way,

But even Doris—I've never found her.

Evening came, a paw, to the gray hut by the
    river.
Pushing the door with a stick, I opened it.
Only a long walk had brought me there,
steps into the continent they had placed before
    me.

I read weathered log, stone fireplace, broken
    chair,
the dead grass outside under the cottonwood
    tree—
and it all stared back. We've met before, my
    memory
started to say, somewhere. . . .

And then I stopped: my father's eyes were gray.

PARENTAGE

My father didn't really belong in history.
He kept looking over his shoulder at some
    mistake.
He was a stranger to me, for I belong.

There never was a particular he couldn't
    understand,
but there were too many in too long a row,
and like many another he was overwhelmed.

Today drinking coffee I look over the cup
and want to have the right amount of fear,
preferring to be saved and not, like him, heroic.

I want to be as afraid as the teeth are big,
I want to be as dumb as the wise are wrong:
I'd just as soon be pushed by events to where I
    belong.

MY FATHER: OCTOBER 1942

He picks up what he thinks is
a road map, and it is
his death: he holds it easily, and
nothing can take it from his firm hand.
The pulse in his thumb on the map
says, "1:19 P.M. next Tuesday, at
this intersection." And an ambulance
begins to throb while his face looks tired.

TROUBLESHOOTING

On still days when country telephone
wires go south, go home, go quietly away into
the woods, a certain little brown bird appears,
hopping and flying by starts, following the line,
trying out each pole.
My father and I, troubleshooting for the
   telephone
company back then, used to see that same bird
along old roads, and it led us to farms
we always thought about owning some day.

When I see that bird now I see my father
tilt his hat and flip the pliers confidently
into the toolbox; the noise of my life, and all
the buffeting from those who judge and pass by,
dwindle off and sink into the silence,
and the little brown bird steadfastly wanders on
pulling what counts wherever it goes.

LIVING ON THE PLAINS

That winter when this thought came—how the
    river
held still every midnight and flowed
backward a minute—we studied algebra
late in our room fixed up in the barn,
and I would feel the curved relation,
the rafters upside down, and the cows in their
    life
holding the earth round and ready
to meet itself again when morning came.

At breakfast while my mother stirred the cereal
she said, "You're studying too hard,"
and I would include her face and hands in my
    glance
and then look past my father's gaze as
he told again our great race through the stars
and how the world can't keep up with our
    dreams.

A CATECHISM

Who challenged my soldier mother?
    Nobody.
Who kept house for her and fended off the
    world?
    My father.
Who suffered most from her oppressions?
    My sister.
Who went out into the world to right its wrongs?
    My sister.
Who became bitter when the world didn't listen?
    My sister.
Who challenged my soldier sister?
    Nobody.
Who grew up and saw all this and recorded it
    and
kept wondering how to solve it but couldn't?
    Guess who.

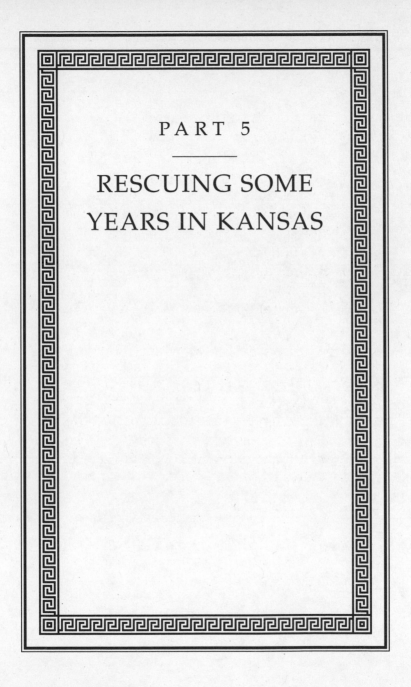

PART 5

RESCUING SOME
YEARS IN KANSAS

THE FARM ON THE GREAT PLAINS

A telephone lines goes cold;
birds tread it wherever it goes.
A farm back of a great plain
tugs an end of the line.

I call that farm every year,
ringing it, listening, still;
no one is home at the farm,
the line gives only a hum.

Some year I will ring the line
on a night at last the right one,
and with an eye tapered for braille
from the phone on the wall

I will see the tenant who waits—
the last one left at the place;
through the dark my braille eye
will lovingly touch his face.

"Hello, is Mother at home?"
No one is home today.
"But Father—he should be there."
No one—no one is here.

"But you—are you the one . . . ?"
Then the line will be gone
because both ends will be home:
no space, no birds, no farm.

My self will be the plain,
wise as winter is gray,
pure as cold posts go
pacing toward what I know.

SERVING WITH GIDEON

Now I remember: in our town the druggist
prescribed Coca-Cola mostly, in tapered
glasses to us, and to the elevator
man in a paper cup, so he could
drink it elsewhere because he was black.

And now I remember the Legion—gambling
in the back room, and no women but girls, old
    boys
who ran the town. They were generous,
to their sons or the sons of friends.
And of course I was almost one.

I remember winter light closing
its great blue fist slowly eastward
along the street, and the dark then, deep
as war, arched over a radio show
called the thirties in the great old U.S.A.

Look down, stars—I was almost
one of the boys. My mother was folding
her handkerchief; the library seethed and
    sparked;
right and wrong arced; and carefully
I walked with my cup toward the elevator man.

THE RESCUED YEAR

Take a model of the world so big
it is the world again, pass your hand,
press back that area in the West where no one
    lived,
the place only your mind explores. On your
    thumb
that smudge becomes my ignorance, a badge
the size of Colorado: toward that state by train
we crossed our state like birds and lodged—
the year my sister gracefully
grew up—against the western boundary
where my father had a job.

Time should go the way it went
that year: we weren't at war; we had
each day a treasured unimportance;
the sky existed, so did our town;
the library had books we hadn't read;
every day at school we learned and sang,
or at least hummed and walked in the hall.

In church I heard the preacher; he said
"Honor!" with a sound like empty silos
repeating the lesson. For a minute I held
Kansas Christian all along the Santa Fe.
My father's mean attention, though, was busy—
    this

I knew—and going home his wonderfully level
    gaze
would hold the state I liked, where little
    happened
and much was understood. I watched my
    father's finger
mark off huge eye-scans of what happened in
    the creed.

Like him, I tried. I still try,
send my sight like a million pickpockets
up rich people's drives; it is time
when I pass for every place I go to be alive.
Around any corner my sight is a river,
and I let it arrive: rich by those brooks
his thought poured for hours
into my hand. His creed: the greatest ownership
of all is to glance around and understand.

That Christmas Mother made paper
presents; we colored them with crayons
and hung up a tumbleweed for a tree.
A man from Hugoton brought my sister
a present (his farm was tilted near oil
wells; his car ignored the little
bumps along our drive: nothing
came of all this—it was just part of the year).

I walked out where a girl I knew would be;
we crossed the plank over the ditch
to her house. There was popcorn on the stove,
and her mother recalled the old days, inviting
    me back.

When I walked home in the cold evening,
snow that blessed the wheat had roved
along the highway seeking furrows,
and all the houses had their lights—
oh, that year did not escape me: I rubbed
the wonderful old lamp of our dull town.

That spring we crossed the state again,
my father soothing us with stories:
the river lost in Utah, underground—
"They've explored only the ones they've found!"—
and that old man who spent his life knowing,
unable to tell how he knew—
"I've been sure by smoke, persuaded
by mist, or a cloud, or a name:
once the truth was ready"—my father smiled
at this—"it didn't care how it came."

In all his ways I hold that rescued year—
comes that smoke like love into the broken
coal, that forms to chunks again and lies
in the earth again in its dim folds, and comes a
    sound,
then shapes to make a whistle fade,
and in the quiet I hold no need, no hurry:
any day the dust will move, maybe settle;
the train that left will roll back into our station,
the name carved on the platform unfill with rain,
and the sound that followed the couplings back
will ripple forward and hold the train.

IN THE DEEP CHANNEL

Setting a trotline after sundown
if we went far enough away in the night
sometimes up out of deep water
would come a secret-headed channel cat,

Eyes that were still eyes in the rush of darkness,
flowing feelers noncommittal and black,
and hidden in the fins those rasping bone
    daggers,
with one spiking upward on its back.

We would come at daylight and find the line sag,
the fishbelly gleam and the rush on the tether:
to feel the swerve and the deep current
which tugged at the tree roots below the river.

Lorene—we thought she'd come home. But
it got late, and then days. Now
it has been years. Why shouldn't she,
if she wanted? I would: something comes
along, a sunny day, you start walking;
you meet a person who says, "Follow me,"
and things lead on.

Usually, it wouldn't happen, but sometimes
the neighbors notice your car is gone, the
patch of oil in the driveway, and it fades.
They forget.

In the Bible it happened—fishermen, Levites.
They just went away and kept going. Thomas,
away off in India, never came back.

But Lorene—it was a stranger maybe, and he
said, "Your life, I need it." And nobody else did.

LOOKING ACROSS THE RIVER

We were driving the river road.
It was at night. "There's the island,"
someone said. And we all looked across
at the light where the hermit lived.

"I'd be afraid to live there"—
it was Ken the driver who spoke.
He shivered and let us feel
the fear that made him shake.

Over to that dark island
my thought had already crossed—
I felt the side of the house
and the night wind unwilling to rest.

For the first time in all my life
I became someone else:
it was dark; others were going their way;
the river and I kept ours.

We came on home that night;
the road led us on. Everything
we said was louder—it was hollow,
and sounded dark like a bridge.

Somewhere I had lost someone—
so dear or so great or so fine
that I never cared again: as if
time dimmed, and color and sound were gone.

Come for me now, World—
whatever is near, come close.
I have been over the water
and lived there all alone.

FIFTEEN

South of the bridge on Seventeenth
I found back of the willows one summer
day a motorcycle with engine running
as it lay on its side, ticking over
slowly in the high grass. I was fifteen.

I admired all that pulsing gleam, the
shiny flanks, the demure headlights
fringed where it lay; I led it gently
to the road and stood with that
companion, ready and friendly. I was fifteen.

We could find the end of a road, meet
the sky on out Seventeenth. I thought about
hills, and patting the handle got back a
confident opinion. On the bridge we indulged
a forward feeling, a tremble. I was fifteen.

Thinking, back farther in the grass I found
the owner, just coming to, where he had flipped
over the rail. He had blood on his hand, was pale—
I helped him walk to his machine. He ran his
   hand
over it, called me good man, roared away.

I stood there, fifteen.

Animals own a fur world;
people own worlds that are variously, pleasingly,
    bare.
And the way these worlds *are* once arrived for us
    kids with a jolt,
that night when the wild woman danced
in the giant cage we found we were all in
at the state fair.

Better women exist, no doubt, than that one,
and occasions more edifying, too, I suppose.
But we have to witness for ourselves what comes
    for us,
nor be distracted by barkers of irrelevant ware;
and a pretty good world, I say, arrived that night
when that woman came farming right out of her
    clothes,
by God,

At the state fair.

REMEMBERING BROTHER BOB

Tell me, you years I had for my life,
tell me a day, that day it snowed
and I played hockey in the cold.
Bob was seven, then, and I was twelve,
and strong. The sun went down. I turned
and Bob was crying on the shore.

Do I remember kindness? Did I
shield my brother, comfort him?
Tell me, you years I had for my life.

Yes, I carried him. I took
him home. But I complained. I see
the darkness; it comes near: and Bob,
who is gone now, and the other kids.
I am the zero in the scene:
"You said you would be brave," I chided
him. "I'll not take you again."
Years, I look at the white across
this page, and think: I never did.

AUNT MABEL

This town is haunted by some good deed
that reappears like a country cousin, or truth
when language falters these days trying to lie,
because Aunt Mabel, an old lady gone now,
    would
accost even strangers to give bright flowers
away, quick as a striking snake. It's deeds like
    this
have weakened me, shaken by intermittent trust,
stricken with friendliness.

Our Senator talked like war, and Aunt Mabel
said, "He's a brilliant man,
but we didn't elect him that much."

Everyone's resolve weakens toward evening
or in a flash when a face melds—a stranger's,
    even—
reminded for an instant between menace and
    fear:
There are Aunt Mabels all over the world,
    or their graves in the rain.

A FAMILY TURN

All her kamikaze friends admired my aunt,
their leader, charmed in vinegar,
a woman who could blaze with such white blasts
as Lawrence's that lit Arabia.
Her mean opinions bent her hatpins.

We'd take a ride in her old car
that ripped like Sherman through society:
Main Street's oases sheltered no one
when she pulled up at Thirty-first
and whirled that Ford for another charge.

We swept headlines from under rugs, names
all over town, which I learned her way, by heart,
and blazed with love that burns because it's real.
With a turn that's our family's own,
she'd say, "Our town is not the same"—

Pause—"And it's never been."

Mine was a midwest home—you can keep your
world.
Plain black hats rode the thoughts that made our
code.
We sang hymns in the house; the roof was near
God.

The light bulb that hung in the pantry made a
wan light,
but we could read by it the names of preserves—
outside, the buffalo grass, and the wind in the
night.

A wildcat sprang at Grandpa on the Fourth of
July
when he was cutting plum bushes for fuel,
before Indians pulled the West over the edge of
the sky.

To anyone who looked at us we said, "My
friend";
liking the cut of a thought, we could say "Hello."
(But plain black hats rode the thoughts that
made our code.)

The sun was over our town; it was like a blade.
Kicking cottonwood leaves we ran toward
   storms.
Wherever we looked the land would hold us up.

In the play Amy didn't want to be
anybody; so she managed the curtain.
Sharon wanted to be Amy. But Sam
wouldn't let anybody be anybody else—
he said it was wrong. "All right," Steve said,
"I'll be me, but I don't like it."
So Amy was Amy, and we didn't have the play.
And Sharon cried.

REMEMBERING

When there was air, when you could
breathe any day if you liked, and if you
wanted to you could run, I used to
climb those hills back of town and
follow a gully so my eyes were at ground
level and could look out through grass as the
  stems
bent in their tensile way, and see snow
mountains follow along, the way distance goes.

Now I carry those days in a tiny box
wherever I go. I open the lid like this
and let the light glimpse and then glance away.
There is a sigh like my breath when I do this.
Some days I do this again and again.

EARTH DWELLER

It was all the clods at once become
precious; it was the barn, and the shed,
and the windmill, my hands, the crack
Arlie made in the ax handle: oh, let me stay
here humbly, forgotten, to rejoice in it all;
let the sun casually rise and set.
If I have not found the right place,
teach me; for, somewhere inside, the clods are
vaulted mansions, lines through the barn sing
for the saints forever, the shed and windmill
rear so glorious the sun shudders like a gong.

Now I know why people worship, carry around
magic emblems, wake up talking dreams
they teach to their children: the world speaks.
The world speaks everything to us.
It is our only friend.

CEREMONY

On the third finger of my left hand
under the bank of the Ninnescah
a muskrat whirled and bit to the bone.
The mangled hand made the water red.

That was something the ocean would remember:
I saw me in the current flowing through the
    land,
rolling, touching roots, the world incarnadined,
and the river richer by a kind of marriage.

While in the woods an owl started quavering
with drops like tears I raised my arm.
Under the bank a muskrat was trembling
with meaning my hand would wear forever.

In that river my blood flowed on.

PRAIRIE TOWN

There was a river under First and Main;
the salt mines honeycombed farther down.
A wealth of sun and wind ever so strong
converged on that home town, long gone.

At the north edge there were the sand hills.
I used to stare for hours at prairie dogs,
which had their town, and folded their little
    paws
to stare beyond their fence where I was.

River rolling in secret, salt mines with care
holding your crystals and stillness, north
    prairie—
what kind of trip can I make, with what old
    friend,
ever to find a town so widely rich again?

Pioneers, for whom history was walking through
    dead grass,
and the main things that happened were miles
    and the time of day—
you built that town, and I have let it pass.
Little folded paws, judge me: I came away.

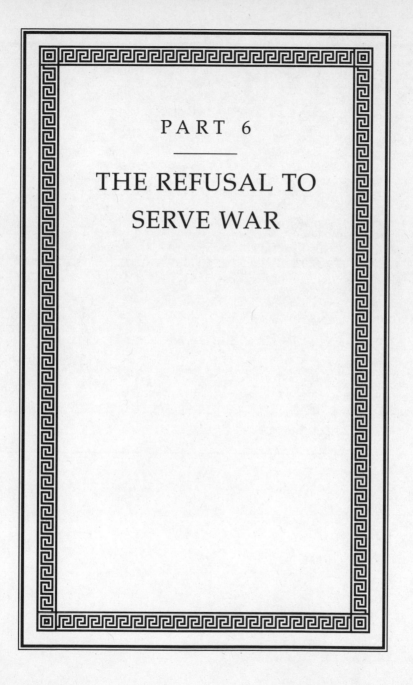

PART 6

THE REFUSAL TO SERVE WAR

We must go back and find a trail on the ground
back of the forest and mountain on the slow
    land;
we must begin to circle on the intricate sod.
By such wild beginnings without help we may
    find
the small trail on through the buffalo-bean vines.

We must go back with noses and the palms of
    our hands,
and climb over the map in far places,
    everywhere,
and lie down whenever there is doubt and sleep
    there.
If roads are unconnected we must make a path,
no matter how far it is, or how lowly we arrive.

We must find something forgotten by everyone
    alive,
and make some fabulous gesture when the sun
    goes down
as they do by custom in little Mexico towns
where they crawl for some ritual up a rocky
    steep.
The jet planes dive; we must travel on our knees.

AT THE BOMB TESTING SITE

At noon in the desert a panting lizard
waited for history, its elbows tense,
watching the curve of a particular road
as if something might happen.

It was looking at something farther off
than people could see, an important scene
acted in stone for little selves
at the flute end of consequences.

There was just a continent without much on it
under a sky that never cared less.
Ready for a change, the elbows waited.
The hands gripped hard on the desert.

CLASH

The butcher knife was there
on the table my father made.
The hatchet was on the stair;
I knew where it was.

Hot wires burned in the wall;
all the nails pointed in.
At the sound of my mother's call
I knew it was the time.

When she threatened I hid in the yard.
Policemen would come for me.
It was dark; waiting was hard.
There was something I had to win.

After my mother wept
I forgot where the hatchet was:
there was a truce we kept—
we both chose real things.

If she taunted, I grew still.
If she faltered, I lowered the knife.
I did not have to kill.
Time had made me stronger.

I won before too late,
and—a man by the time she died—
I had traveled from love to hate
and partway back again.

Now all I have, my life,
strange, comes partly from this:
I thought about a knife
when I learned that great word—"Choose."

A DEDICATION

We stood by the library. It was an August night.
Priests and sisters of hundreds of unsaid creeds
passed us going their separate pondered roads.
We watched them cross under the corner light.

Freights on the edge of town were carrying away
flatcars of steel to be made into secret guns;
we knew, being human, that they were enemy
    guns,
and we were somehow vowed to poverty.

No one stopped or looked long or held out a
    hand.
They were following orders received from hour
    to hour,
so many signals, all strange, from a foreign
    power:
But tomorrow, you whispered, *peace may flow over
    the land.*

At that corner in a flash of lightning we two
    stood;
that glimpse we had will stare through the dark
    forever:

on the poorest roads we would be walkers and
   beggars,
toward some deathless meeting involving a crust
   of bread.

MR. OR MRS. NOBODY

Some days when you look out, the land
is heavy, following its hills, dim
where a road bends. There are days when
having the world is a mistake.
But then you think, "Well, anyway, it wasn't
my idea," and it's OK again.

Suppose that a person who knows you happens
to see you going by, and it's one of those days—
for a minute you have to carry the load
for them, you've got to lift the whole
heavy world, even without knowing it,
being a hero, stumbling along.
Some days it's like that. And maybe
today. And maybe all of the time.

In line at lunch I cross my fork and spoon
to ward off complicity—the ordered life
our leaders have offered us. Thin as a knife,
our chance to live depends on such a sign
while others talk and the Pentagon from the
    moon
is bouncing exact commands: "Forget your faith;
be ready for whatever it takes to win: we face
annihilation unless all citizens get in line."

I bow and cross my fork and spoon: somewhere
other citizens more fearfully bow
in a place terrorized by their kind of oppressive
    state.
Our signs both mean, "You hostages over there
will never be slaughtered by my act." Our vows
cross: never to kill and call it fate.

AT THE UN-NATIONAL MONUMENT
ALONG THE CANADIAN BORDER

This is the field where the battle did not happen,
where the unknown soldier did not die.
This is the field where grass joined hands,
where no monument stands,
and the only heroic thing is the sky.

Birds fly here without any sound,
unfolding their wings across the open.
No people killed—or were killed—on this
    ground
hallowed by neglect and an air so tame
that people celebrate it by forgetting its name.

FOR MY YOUNG FRIENDS WHO ARE
AFRAID

There is a country to cross you will
find in the corner of your eye, in
the quick slip of your foot—air far
down, a snap that might have caught.
And maybe for you, for me, a high, passing
voice that finds its way by being
afraid. That country is there, for us,
carried as it is crossed. What you fear
will not go away: it will take you into
yourself and bless you and keep you.
That's the world, and we all live there.

HOW IT IS

It is war. They put us on a train and
say, "Go." A bell wakes up the engine
as we move along past the crowd,
and a child—one clear small gaze from all the
    town—
finds my face. I wave. For long I look
back. "I'm not a soldier," I want to say.
But the gaze is left behind. And I'm gone.

It is August. Your father is walking you
to the train for camp and then the War
and on out of his life, but you don't know.

Little lights along the path glow under their
    hoods
and your shoes go brown, brown in the
    brightness
till the next interval, when they disappear in the
    shadow.

You know they are down there, by the crunch of
    stone
and a rustle when they touch a fern. Somewhere
    above,
cicadas arch their gauze of sound all over town.

Shivers of summer wind follow across the park
and then turn back. You walk on toward
September, the depot, the dark, the light, the
    dark.

IN CAMP

That winter of the war, every day
sprang outward. I was a prisoner.
Someone brought me gifts. That year
now is far: birds can't fly
the miles to find a forgotten cause.

No task I do today has justice
at the end. All I know is
my degree of leaning in this wind
where—once the mind springs free—
every cause has reason
but reason has no law.

In camps like that, if I should go again,
I'd still study the gospel and play the accordion.

TIME CAPSULE

That year the news
was a storm, a wind that
puzzled monuments. Wrecks piled up
on the coast, and at year's end
after the party and song we sang
our old composition called "Friend,"
wrapped up the scraps for the stock;
then one by one
through perspective we took up coat
and hat and
were gone,
westward up the river
where flood-mangled cottonwoods
imitated grotesquely Governor
and President and Saint, bend by
bend, all the way home.

That year the news was
not only free, it was mandatory.
The barometer said "War."
To the west gulls came
in like tracers.

Back on the farm it was calm,
and pigs ate the greasy newspapers.

MEDITATION

Animals full of light
walk through the forest
toward someone aiming a gun
loaded with darkness.

That's the world: God
holding still
letting it happen again,
and again and again.

PEACE WALK

We wondered what our walk should mean,
taking that un-march quietly;
the sun stared at our signs—"Thou shalt not
    kill."

Men by a tavern said, "Those foreigners . . . "
to a woman with a fur, who turned away—
like an elevator going down, their look at us.

Along a curb, their signs lined across,
a picket line stopped and stared
the whole width of the street, at ours: "Unfair."

Above our heads the sound truck blared—
by the park, under the autumn trees—
it said that love could fill the atmosphere:

Occur, slow the other fallout, unseen,
on islands everywhere—fallout, falling
unheard. We held our poster up to shade our
    eyes.

At the end we just walked away;
no one was there to tell us where to leave the
    signs.

IN THE WHITE SKY

Many things in the world have
already happened. You can
go back and tell about them.
They are part of what we
own as we speed along
through the white sky.

But many things in the world
haven't yet happened. You help
them by thinking and writing and acting.
Where they begin, you greet them
or stop them. You come along
and sustain the new things.

Once in the white sky there was
a beginning, and I happened to notice
and almost glimpsed what to do.
But now I have come far
to here, and it is away back there.
Some days, I think about it.

ASK ME

Some time when the river is ice ask me
mistakes I have made. Ask me whether
what I have done is my life. Others
have come in their slow way into
my thought, and some have tried to help
or to hurt: ask me what difference
their strongest love or hate has made.

I will listen to what you say.
You and I can turn and look
at the silent river and wait. We know
the current is there, hidden; and there
are comings and goings from miles away
that hold the stillness exactly before us.
What the river says, that is what I say.

Ants, when they meet each other,
usually pass on the right.

Sometimes you can open a sticky
door with your elbow.

A man in Boston has dedicated himself
to telling about injustice.
For three thousand dollars he will
come to your town and tell you about it.

Schopenhauer was a pessimist but
he played the flute.

Yeats, Pound, and Eliot saw art as
growing from other art. They studied that.

If I ever die, I'd like it to be
in the evening. That way, I'll have
all the dark to go with me, and no one
will see how I begin to hobble along.

In the Pentagon one person's job is to
take pins out of towns, hills, and fields,
and then save the pins for later.

THE STAR IN THE HILLS

A star hit in the hills behind our house
up where the grass turns brown touching the
    sky.

Meteors have hit the world before, but this was
    near,
and since TV; few saw, but many felt the shock.
The state of California owns that land
(and out from shore three miles), and any stars
that come will be roped off and viewed on
    weekdays 8 to 5.

A guard who took the oath of loyalty and denied
any police record told me this:
"If you don't have a police record yet
you could take the oath and get a job
if California should be hit by another star."

"I'd promise to be loyal to California
and to guard any stars that hit it," I said,
"or any place three miles out from shore,
unless the star was bigger than the state—
in which case I'd be loyal to *it*."

But he said no exceptions were allowed,
and he leaned against the state-owned meteor
so calm and puffed a cork-tip cigarette
that I looked down and traced with my foot in
    the dust
and thought again and said, "OK—any star."

SO LONG

At least at night, a streetlight
is better than a star.
And better good shoes on a
long walk than a good friend.

Often in winter with my old
cap I slip away into the gloom
like a happy fish, at home
with all I touch, at the level of love.

No one can surface till far,
far on, and all that we'll have
to love may be what's near
in the cold, even then.

It is people at the edge who say
things at the edge: winter is toward knowing.

    Sled runners before they meet have long talk
      apart.
    There is a pup in every litter the wolves will
      have.
    A knife that falls points at an enemy.
    Rocks in the wind know their place: down
      low.
    Over your shoulder is God; the dying deer
      sees Him.

At the mouth of the long sack we fall in forever
storms brighten the spikes of the stars.

    Wind that buried bear skulls north of here
    and beats moth wings for help outside the
      door
    is bringing bear skull wisdom, but do not ask
      the skull
    too large a question till summer.
    Something too dark was held in that strong
      bone.

Better to end with a lucky saying:

Sled runners cannot decide to join or to part.
When they decide, it is a bad day.

PURIFYING THE LANGUAGE OF THE TRIBE

Walking away means
"Goodbye."

Pointing a knife at your stomach means
"Please don't say that again."

Leaning toward you means
"I love you."

Raising a finger means
"I enthusiastically agree."

"Maybe" means
"No."

"Yes" means
"Maybe."

Looking like this at you means
"You had your chance."

THE WELL RISING

The well rising without sound,
the spring on a hillside,
the plowshare brimming through deep ground
everywhere in the field—

The sharp swallows in their swerve
flaring and hesitating
hunting for the final curve
coming closer and closer—

The swallow heart from wingbeat to wingbeat
counseling decision, decision:
thunderous examples. I place my feet
with care in such a world.

A RITUAL TO READ TO EACH OTHER

If you don't know the kind of person I am
and I don't know the kind of person you are
a pattern that others made may prevail in the
    world
and following the wrong god home we may miss
    our star.

For there is many a small betrayal in the mind,
a shrug that lets the fragile sequence break
sending with shouts the horrible errors of
    childhood
storming out to play through the broken dike.

And as elephants parade holding each
    elephant's tail,
but if one wanders the circus won't find the
    park,
I call it cruel and maybe the root of all cruelty
to know what occurs but not recognize the fact.

And so I appeal to a voice, to something
    shadowy,
a remote important region in all who talk:
though we could fool each other, we should
    consider—

lest the parade of our mutual life get lost in the
  dark.

For it is important that awake people be awake,
or a breaking line may discourage them back to
  sleep;
the signals we give—yes or no, or maybe—
should be clear: the darkness around us is deep.

INDEX

Adults Only, 96
Allegiances, 30
Any Time, 10
Archival Print, An, 25
Ask Me, 126
At Our House, 5
At the Bomb Testing Site, 110
At the Un-National Monument
   Along the Canadian Border, 117
Aunt Mabel, 98

Bi-Focal, 17
By a River in the Osage Country,
   45

Catechism, A, 82
Ceremony, 105
Clash, 111
Concealment, The: Ishi, the Last
   Wild Indian, 51
Consolations, 6

Dedication, A, 113

Earth Dweller, 104
108 East 19th, 71

Fall Journey, 77
Family Turn, A, 99
Farm on the Great Plains, The, 85
Father's Voice, 72
Fifteen, 95
First Grade, 102
For a Lost Child, 7
For My Young Friends Who Are

Afraid, 118
Found in a Storm, 21
From the Move to California, 28

How It Is, 119
How These Words Happened, 19
How to Regain Your Soul, 31

If I Could Be Like Wallace Stevens,
   23
In Camp, 121
Indian Caves in the Dry Country,
   47
In Fur, 46
In the Deep Channel, 91
In the Night Desert, 44
In the Oregon Country, 41
In the White Sky, 125

Light by the Barn, The, 9
Listening, 74
Living on the Plains, 81
Long Distance, 12
Looking Across the River, 93

Meditation, 123
Memorial, A: Son Bret, 8
Mother's Day, 68
Mr. or Mrs. Nobody, 115
My Father: October 1942, 79
My Hands, 24
My Mother Was a Soldier, 66

Near, 20
1940, 120

Objector, 116
One Home, 100
Oregon Message, An, 29
Our Kind, 65

Parentage, 78
Passing Remark, 4
Peace Walk, 124
People of the South Wind, 53
Prairie Town, 106
Purifying the Language of the Tribe,
  133

Remembering, 103
Remembering Brother Bob, 97
Report to Crazy Horse, 55
Rescued Year, The, 88
Research Team in the Mountains,
  The, 59
Returned to Say, 48
Ritual to Read to Each Other, A,
  135
Run Before Dawn, 26

Saint Matthew and All, 92
Salvaged Parts, 32
Sayings from the Northern Ice, 131
Serving with Gideon, 87
Sioux Haiku, 58

So Long, 130
Some Shadows, 69
Song in the Manner of Flannery
  O'Connor, A, 22
Star in the Hills, The, 128
Stories to Live in the World With,
  42
Story That Could Be True, A, 18

Thanksgiving for My Father, A, 75
Things I Learned Last Week, 127
Thinking for Berky, 37
Time Capsule, 122
Traveling Through the Dark, 36
Troubleshooting, 80
Turn Over Your Hand, 33

Ultimate Problems, 61

Vacation Trip, 67
Vocation, 73

Waiting in Line, 34
Watching the Jet Planes Dive, 109
Weather Report, 62
Well Rising, The, 134
Wind World, 49
With Kit, Age Seven, at the Beach, 3